T0102485

Ross's

Key Discoveries

Michael Ross

Ross's

Key Discoveries

Michael Ross

Rare Bird • Los Angeles, Calif.

THIS IS A GENUINE RARE BIRD BOOK

A Rare Bird Book | Rare Bird Books
6044 North Figueroa Street
Los Angeles, CA 90042
rarebirdbooks.com

FIRST HARDCOVER EDITION

Set in Minion
Printed in the United States
Distributed worldwide by Publishers Group West

Publisher's Cataloging-in-Publication Data
Names: Ross, Michael, author.
Title: Ross's Key Discoveries / Michael Ross.
Series: Ross's Quotations.
Description: First Hardcover Edition | A Genuine Rare Bird Book | New York, NY;
Los Angeles, CA: Rare Bird Books, 2022.
Identifiers: ISBN 9781644282434
Subjects: LCSH Communication—Quotations, maxims, etc. | Quotations, English. |
BISAC REFERENCE / Quotations
Classification: LCC PN90 .R67 2019 | DDC 302.2—dc23

With thanks for all the personal and professional experiences that gave me lessons about money, wisdom, and happiness.

Introduction

As I offer the seventh volume of quotes from those I have collected since the seventies, I hope that I should not need to say too much about my experience reading literary fiction. Much of it has been described in detail in the introductions to the first six volumes. Suffice it, I hope, to say that I continue to read a variety of classic, modern, and contemporary fiction, including drama and short stories. I am trying to broaden my sources to include more female and foreign authors, especially winners of the Nobel Prize for Literature. I still enjoy reading books set in places where I am traveling, recently, *The President* by Miguel Angel Asturias and *God's Favorite* by Lawrence Wright, while I was in Central America. This is a practice I highly recommend to enhance a travel experience whether near or far. I usually read two or more books contemporaneously, so I am sure to have something satisfying to read. The increase in the number of authors is intended not only to enhance my experience and enjoyment, but also to offer more variety for my readers. I am no longer fixated on finishing every book I begin, and I am, therefore, collecting more unfinished books. Among the books I finish, I find many excellent ones give me few or no quotes for my collection, while others provide many. I try not to select authors and books for any perceived likelihood of finding collectible quotes.

I selected the topics for this volume—money, wisdom, and happiness—because they are among the common goals for many people. They are also somewhat related to each other. More important, all three are interesting subjects.

Money, wealth, and the lack thereof receive a great deal of attention, not just in literary fiction, but also in all sorts of nonfiction books and numerous well-meaning articles. There are those that focus on the wealthy, the extremely wealthy, the "one percent," and the top one-tenth of one percent. Others describe the poor, very poor, and destitute at home and abroad.

One interesting phenomenon is that some people who have, one way or another, accumulated substantial wealth feel they have also acquired wisdom about subjects wholly unrelated to the means by which they achieved that wealth. Less fortunate people often tend to accept pronouncements, without serious question, of such purported experience by the wealthy.

An intriguing issue about money is figuring out how much is enough. For some people there seems never to be enough. Others find they have plenty and give, or promise to give, away large amounts of their wealth to charitable causes. In the introduction to John Bogle's book *Enough*, he relates the story about a billionaire's party at which Kurt Vonnegut tells Joseph Heller that their host has made more money in a single day than Heller earned from his novel *Catch-22*. Heller responds by saying that he has something the billionaire would never have—"enough."

An obvious and frequently asked question is if money will "buy" happiness for those who have it. A corollary question asks if those without some amount of money are destined to be unhappy.

Many of us strive to be wise, for wisdom's sake alone or because we think it will help us make money or be happy. In any case, it would be useful to know what wisdom is and how we might efficiently obtain it. Again, there is no dearth of nonfiction advising us what and how we may learn about myriad topics in a wide variety of fields, such as history, science, psychology, health, and government. Even if we immerse ourselves in studying our chosen subjects, how would we know when or if we have attained wisdom? Shakespeare offers us an ironic truth in Act V, Scene I of *All's Well That Ends Well*: "The fool doth think he is wise, but the wise man knows himself to be a fool." He offers proof in the relative positions of King Lear and his "fool."

Assuming we were somehow able to know that we had achieved some level of wisdom (possibly through our wisdom, if that is not too circular), would wisdom alone be enough? In I Corinthians 13, verse 2, Paul writes: "If I have prophetic powers, and understand all mysteries...but have not love, I am nothing." So, from the theological perspective, obtaining all the wisdom in the world would not be worth the proverbial "candle." Nonetheless, some wisdom about, for example, how much money is enough would seem to be valuable.

What makes us happy? An easier question is to ask what makes us unhappy. The causes are legion, including only a short list: illness, pain, being treated unfairly, being betrayed, a loved ones' terminal illness or death, and frustrated hopes and dreams. Again, there is no shortage of nonfiction written on these topics, and psychologists, psychiatrists, counselors, and life coaches all want to help us. So does big pharma by selling numerous drugs to combat depression and less serious unhappy conditions.

The sources of happiness may be significant events, such as, an engagement, wedding, birth of a healthy child, receipt of an honor or award or a promotion. Some conditions may also give us a different sort of happiness if we take time to consider them, such as, good health, loving family members, loyal friends, and attractive surroundings. Proverbial "little things" may cause us spurts of happiness, like a home team's win, an especially tasty meal, or a beautiful sunrise or sunset. In a sense, these are all external sources, but philosophers tell us that much depends on our own feelings and thinking. Descartes put it simply: "try always to conquer myself rather than fortune, and to alter my desires rather than change the order of the world, and generally to accustom myself to believe that there is nothing entirely within our power but our own thoughts."

After publishing six earlier parts of my collection of quotes, I remain committed to the value of quotes, and I hope to publish future volumes that would include quotes about the arts, God, faith and religion, fate, death, law, justice, honesty, and government. Some quotes are educational, some are provocative, some are humorous, and some are all three. They can confirm what we believe or think (which reminds me of a bumper sticker warning that we need not believe everything we think) or hope, or they can disabuse of notions we should abandon. I hope the quotes in my collection will introduce readers to authors and books they might enjoy.

Money

There is no shortage of writing about money; there are myriad books and articles on finance for the young, old, and middle aged. The topics include how to earn or otherwise get it, how to invest it wisely, and how to avoid mistakes planning for retirement. Society applauds the wealthy, the rich, and the "one percent." The assumption, whether stated or not, is that having some amount of money will make us happy. Although having enough to live reasonably well is a worthwhile goal, how much is enough? I recall one of my first experiences with someone who was wealthy that showed me that money alone was not enough. This college student had inherited substantial wealth, and his lifestyle showed it. He was unhappy, however, in part because he could not tell if his peers liked him or his money.

Poor or Rich

How does money or the lack thereof affect
people, for better or worse?

«»

*The poor know boredom but always hope
that things will change for the better,
whereas the rich simply want things to go
on just as they are, which is even less likely
to happen.*

John Updike, Villages

This sentiment was expressed by a young lady when she expected that she and her betrothed would be poor, and only a short time before they had a windfall of wealth. So, she probably changed her mind about the possibility of happiness and wealth.

«»

"If you're poor, you enjoy occasional treats. If you're rich, you just get bored with pleasure."

P. G. Wodehouse, Sam the Sudden

There is an irony described here that captures how rich and poor people may feel about their money.

«»

Isn't it funny how people who don't have much like to give some of it away? They must like to show what they can do, and how could they show it better than by being kind?

Bertolt Brecht, *The Good Woman of Setzuan*

Some have wealth but want to hide it.
Others do not have it and want to
hide that, too.

《》

*"Like many filthy rich people, I tend to cry
poor,...Never believe people who tell you
they have no money....People who don't
have it seldom mention the fact. People who
do, tend to be embarrassed about it, and so
deny it ."*

Madeleine L'Engle, A House Like
a Lotus

There may well be a "slippery slope"
causing the wealthy to seek perennially to
find something to buy with their money.

«»

*...the financier having enjoyed himself so
thoroughly looked for something to buy in
that curious tradition of the rich who in a
state of general good feeling cast about for
something to buy.*

Jim Harrison, "Legends of the Fall" in
Legends of the Fall

I like this very concise and perceptive
description of one of the common
effects of being rich.

«»

The lives of the rich were hard to imagine;
they involved a lot of not being home.

John Updike, Villages

Here is something positive to be said
about the rich, in this case their being
comfortable falling asleep in a concert.
It may be a bit of an exaggeration.

«»

They have an easy conscience, the rich.
Henry Miller, *Tropic of Cancer*

These characteristics are reasons, in addition to what wealth generally affords, for aspiring to be rich.

《》

What I like about the rich is the freedom and friendliness.

Joyce Cary, *The Horse's Mouth*

Here is wise advice about how we might take good advantage of whatever financial resources we have.

«»

To be rich is not to have one or ten thousand a year, but to be able to get out of that one or ten thousand all that every pound, and every shilling, and every penny will give you.

Anthony Trollope, *The Claverings*

Negative Effects

Money can become the means for some people to get others to do whatever they want, whether for good or evil.

«»

Money is your best tool. Men love money more than country, wife, mistress, perversion, reputation, or, in some cases, life itself.

John Hersey, *Conspiracy*

This brief condemnation of money seems
to be an exaggeration.

«»

*"All money is dirty. If it were clean nobody
would want it."*

Carlos Ruiz Zafón, The Angel's Game

The sense of this succinct observation is that one person's having money and the other's not having it may prevent a healthy relationship.

«»

"Money is a great bar to intimacy."

Louis Auchincloss, "The Lotos Eaters," in *Tales of Yesteryear*

Now, for a much longer exploration of
the potential adverse effects in society
of an over-emphasis on the pursuit of
money. Although this book was published
more than three decades ago, the quote is
still relevant.

«»

And whenever there is more money to be made from money than from anything else, the energies of the state are likely to be devoted increasingly to the production of money, for which there is no community need, to the exclusion of those commodities that are required for health, physical well-being, and contemplation. Whenever there is more money than products to buy with money, much money will be spent to buy more money. Banking will wax predominant, the number of lawyers and accountants will increase, and the society will become disorganized and weak militarily.

Joseph Heller, Picture This

As with many quotes and adages, there is some truth to this one. The salient point is made with the final words, "as such."

«»

"No sane person is interested in money as such."

> Sloan Wilson, *The Man In the Gray Flannel Suit*

Here is another uncharitable commentary on money, asserting that excess attention to getting or keeping it can be ruinous.

«»

"Money is like any other virus: once it has rotted the soul of the person who houses it, it sets off in search of new blood."

Carlos Ruiz Zafón, *The Shadow of the Wind*

If you think money is dirty, you will like
this emphatic exhortation.

«»

*Go back for enough and all the money
stinks, is dirty, roils the juices of the jaw.
Was there any clean money on earth? Had
there ever been any? No. Categorically.*

Martin Amis, London Fields

We might question how common this vice is, but few will question its inclusion among a list of vices.

«»

Greed has always struck me as one of the most readily identifiable human vices and I'd spent far too long as its victim.

Jim Harrison, *The Road Home*

One of my favorite authors uses a powerful (excuse the pun) simile to warn about the potential for money to harm us.

«»

"In many ways money is as dangerous to handle as gun powder."

Joseph Conrad, "The Planter of Malata" in *Within the Tides*

This is a very perceptive observation about how it is not so much about money but what it might accomplish, for good or evil.

«»

Money is never anything but a fantasy currency: it doesn't exist.

Doris Lessing, The Four-Gated City

Positive Effects

Money may, and often does, offer benefits
for many people that should not
be ignored.

«»

*"Money is protection, a cloak; it can buy one
quiet, and some sort of dignity."*

Willa Cather, *My Mortal Enemy*

Here is a very descriptive metaphor for how beneficial money can be.

«»

Money makes you live longer. It seeps into the bloodstream, into the veins and capillaries.

Don DeLillo, "Hammer and Sickle" in *The Angel Esmeralda: Nine Stories*

For those who need money to support a family, it is, obviously, very important.

«»

When you come right down to it, a man with three children has no damn right to say that money doesn't matter.

Sloan Wilson, *The Man In the Gray Flannel Suit*

For the central character in this novel, the effort to make money had become a very fulfilling part of his life, but would later become insufficient to make him content.

«»

In some ways, he loved money; he certainly loved the sedative effects of pursuing it, and if that was all money did for him at this point, it had much to be said for it.

Thomas McGuane, *Nothing but Blue Skies*

The main character is this classic novel struggles in his efforts to make enough to survive and to deal with others who have been more fortunate financially.

《 》

...for human life hangs together with the aid of money, and some people consider that money is the only thing that governs it, either by being none at all or enough, or by being somewhere in between.

Halldor Laxness, Independent People

It seems hard to quarrel with this concise conclusion; whether it refers to having or not having money.

«»

"Money is a very important thing."

Willa Cather, A Lost Lady

Here is a bit more of a philosophical
approach to being comfortable with the
amount of money one has.

«»

*"That is what money is for, to spend and
enjoy life. It's the* idea *of money, getting rid
of the* idea *of money that'll be tough....If
you can spend money and forget about it,
you're safe."*

John O'Hara, The Instrument

This quote, from one of my favorite authors, is a nice follow-up to the preceding quote, showing that it may be possible to have money and not be obsessed by it.

«»

The real advantage of the money was not that it had bought him things: it was the fact that it had allowed him to stop thinking about money.

Paul Auster, *The Music of Chance*

The same author in a more recent novel
has his character expound on this idea
after he unexpectedly received funds that
will support him.

«»

...relieved him of the obligation to think about money seven hundred and forty-six time a day, which in the end was just about as bad if not worse than not having enough money, for those thoughts could be excruciating and even murderous, and not having to think them anymore was a blessing. That was the one true advantage of having money over not having money, he decided—not that you could buy more things with it but that you no longer had to walk around with that infernal thought bubble hanging over your head.

Paul Auster, 4 3 2 1

Wisdom

Another goal for many people is wisdom. Who among us would not wish to be wise? We first have to discern what wisdom is and what it is not, which may not be as easy as it sounds. If we were successful, we could proceed to determining where and how to discover and absorb it. And, if successful on that score, would wisdom alone be satisfying, or do we expect or at least hope, that wisdom will give us something more?

What It Is Not

We are often counseled to know and learn from our past because doing so will enable us to act wisely in the present and future. Here, however, is a suggestion that being captive to our past will not do the trick.

«»

Wallowing in the past may be good literature. As wisdom, it's hopeless.

Aldous Huxley, *The Genius and the Goddess*

Whether our journey involves good or bad luck, there is always the chance of making an unwise decision that will adversely affect our future.

At the bottom of every piece of ill luck there's the wrong choice, the slip of the will that opens the door to disaster.

John Dos Passos, *The Great Days: A Novel*

With his usual irony and sense of humor, this playwright suggests by negative implication that caution and discipline might lead us to wisdom.

«»

I can resist anything except temptation.

Oscar Wilde, *Lady Windermere's Fan*

Once having adopted some false notion,
we can become entrenched in it and
unable to learn the truth.

«»

*Because people cling to folly as if it were
their most prized possession, defending
it, sometimes with violence, against the
possibility of wisdom.*

Richard Russo, "Intervention" in
Trajectory

We are often advised that numbers can be
made to lie and statistics used or misused
to prove whatever the advocate wants.

«»

*"Nothing will ever convince me that wisdom
lies in statistics."*

Carlos Fuentes, The Eagle's Throne

What It Is

In our complex world and among often contradictory experiences, discovering meaningful truths can be challenging.

«»

And none of this, in my opinion, meant anything more than that the world is richer in associations than in meanings, and that it is the part of wisdom to distinguish between the two.

John Barth, Letters

We routinely encounter numerous theories to explain life. Adopting the correct ones is critical.

«»

...that's the good thing about theory: you always have the last word, and in the midst of total destruction, theory remains intact— only the right one, of course.

Günter Grass, *Too Far Afield*

45

Again, the playwright converts, with irony and humor, what may seem to be errors in our ways into something valuable.

《》

Experience is the name everyone gives to their mistakes.

Oscar Wilde, Lady Windermere's Fan

The main character is this extraordinary
novel muses about the course of his life
and criticizes how luck pervades society.

«»

*And so my luck became my wisdom (as the
luck of the damned human race becomes
its wisdom and gets into the books and is
taught in schools).*

Robert Penn Warren, *All the King's Men*

Here we have instructive examples of
how the wise and not so wise
conduct their lives.

«◊»

*"The wise man knows…for he has made up
his mind what will happen, and goes about
to cause it to happen. It is only the fool who
trusts to chance and waits for circumstances
to develop themselves."*

W. Somerset Maugham, *The Making
of a Saint*

We can all recall times when we thought
we had found true meaning in something
and later discovered it needed to be put
into the context of succeeding events.

《》

*...meaning is never in the event but in the
motion through event.*

Robert Penn Warren, *All the King's Men*

How to Obtain It

A means to achieving wisdom may
be through academic or other formal
education. Some of it might be
from professors.

«»

*In a university you cannot get rid of a
tenured professor without an unholy row,
and though academics love bickering,
they hate rows....It was simply that he was
intolerable, and for some reason that is
never accepted as an excuse for getting rid
of anybody.*

Robertson Davies, *The Rebel Angels*

Here is a more concise, and somewhat humorous, commentary on professors.

«»

"It isn't easy to fire a professor that has a beard."

John O'Hara, *The Instrument*

According to this character, there are
some limits to the value of learning.

《》

"*Learning, for its own winsome, perverse
self—hug it to you but keep a club handy.
It is the most entertaining of all mistresses,
and the least to be trusted.*

"*Particularly must one avoid the supersti-
tion that there is some mystical virtue in
erudition.*"

Sinclair Lewis, World So Wide

As an avid reader, I like this suggestion of an alternative to formal education.

«»

I began to develop a firm conviction that most efforts to teach people things were wasted. All they needed was to go off some quiet place and read.

Richard Russo, *The Risk Pool*

Here is another commentary, with a vivid metaphor, on reading as a means of learning things, arguing that the exercise is a personal one.

«◇»

"You can learn almost everything from reading...The same method doesn't work for everyone, each person has to invent his or her own, whichever suits them best, some people spend their entire lives reading but never get beyond reading the words on the page, they don't understand that the words are merely stepping stones placed across a fast-flowing river, and the reason they're there is so that we can reach the farther shore, it's the other side that matters."

José Saramago, *The Cave*

Studying seemed critical for this professional singer, but it may also be so for many vocations and avocations. I like the humorous second thought.

«»

In his line, people keep studying until they die. And maybe even night school, after that.

Richard Powers, *The Time of Our Singing*

For some people there may be limits to the effectiveness of education.

«»

Education had not entirely elevated my concerns in life. It had probably not even assisted my analyses of these concerns, though that was the most I could hope for.

Lorrie Moore, *A Gate At the Stairs*

Could education, formal or otherwise,
really be counterproductive to
obtaining wisdom?

«»

*...education does not really alter character,
but merely intensifies it, making foolish
people more foolish, superstitious people
more superstitious and, of course, wise
people wiser. But the wise are few and lonely.*

Robertson Davies, The Papers of Samuel
Marchbanks

Experience, in contrast to formal education, may be effective.

«»

Thus he started his education, that marvelous, growing, aching process whereby a mind develops into a usable instrument with a collection of proved experience from which to function.

James A. Michener, *Hawaii*

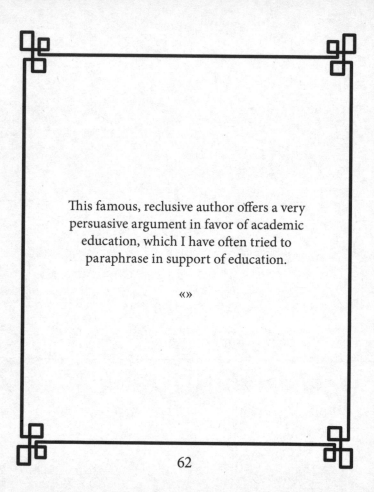

This famous, reclusive author offers a very persuasive argument in favor of academic education, which I have often tried to paraphrase in support of education.

《》

"Something else an academic education will do for you. If you go along with it any considerable distance, it'll begin to give you an idea what size mind you have. What it'll fit and, maybe, what it won't. After a while, you'll have an idea what kind of thoughts your particular size mind should be wearing. For one thing, it may save you an extraordinary amount of time trying on ideas that don't suit you, aren't becoming to you. You'll begin to know your true measurements and dress your mind accordingly."

J. D. Salinger, The Catcher in the Rye

Perhaps, wisdom is something that simply
comes to us at some point in our life,
if we are lucky.

«»

*"Wisdom is sometimes given to the young,
as well as the old."*

James Fenimore Cooper, *The Last of
the Mohicans*

These thoughtful and very positive proposals for a path to wisdom sound so easy but may be difficult to follow.

«»

I had arrived at the summit of wisdom, the point aimed at by the wise man, to take the day as it comes, seizing the pleasures, avoiding the disagreeable, enjoying the present, and giving no thought to the past or future.

W. Somerset Maugham, *The Making of a Saint*

Here is another recipe for finding wisdom.
Can we follow this suggestion?

«»

*To him wisdom consisted in the conscious
and joyous obedience to natural laws.*

Paul Bowles, *The Spider's House*

This quote from a favorite author recalls
the earlier one from Oscar Wilde about
the effects of our experiences.

«»

*At fifty he was perhaps rather old to be
coming to such conclusions, but we all
subscribe thoughtlessly to many beliefs,
the truth of which does not strike home
to us until experience gives them reality.
Wisdom may be rented, so to speak, on the
experience of other people, but we buy it at
an inordinate price before we make it our
own forever.*

Robertson Davies, Leaven of Malice

Even though wisdom may be found
among the generally accepted adages in
our society, it may elude us.

«»

*As that never sufficiently praised popular
wisdom teaches us, and as has more than
once been shown, god writes straight on
crooked lines, and even seems to prefer
the latter.*

José Saramago, *The Elephant's Journey*

Here is a counterpoint to the first wisdom
quote about not finding wisdom in our
past.

«»

*...There is a wisdom in our past that
cannot be approached but with the past's
appurtenances.*

Ken Kesey, Demon Box

The author offers us some very sound ideas about how to achieve true wisdom.

«»

It is one thing, perhaps the wisest, to learn to live with the tight fit and fashion of humility by birth and by station, to accept, with all possible cheerfulness, those things which are not so much earned as given, because with the gift of them no choice is also given to do anything else but, perhaps, to elect to deceive yourself by the folly of denial. Acceptance (thy will be done), then, of what you have been given, both blessings and curses, being, you like to think, the source of the strength and wisdom of humility.

George Garrett, *Entered From the Sun*

Reaching a state of wisdom may require
living through some rough spots.

«◊»

*"One cannot even try to be wise who has
not made a fool of himself, lost friends,
compromised, had the shame of telling
lies—as we all do, we all do."*

John Hersey, The Conspiracy

We would usually consider ignorance the complete lack of wisdom, but ignorance may offer an ironic benefit.

«»

...one good thing about ignorance, it protects us from false knowledge.

José Saramago, The Elephant's Journey

Even our ignorance, that is, a lack of wisdom, may offer long-term knowledge if we acknowledge our errors.

«»

Ignorance ironically arranged for future self-knowledge. Life was never perfect.

Lorrie Moore, "Wings" in *Bark: Stories*

Here are some specific and well-considered recommendations for how we can discover wisdom.

«»

"The world is hard and cruel. We are here none knows why, and we go none knows whither. We must be very humble. We must see the beauty of quietness. We must go through life so inconspicuously that Fate does not notice us. And let us seek the love of simple, ignorant people. Their ignorance is better than all our knowledge. Let us be silent, content in our little corner, meek and gentle like them. That is the wisdom of life."

W. Somerset Maugham, *The Moon and Sixpence*

Happiness

We often say to others and ourselves that all we want is to be happy, and that all we want for our family members is for them to be happy. Has our society over-emphasized the pursuit of happiness, diminishing other worthy goals, such as, morality, compassion, and duty? Although there is more to a meaningful life than simply some degree of happiness, happiness, however we define it, is a much sought-after commodity. So, we will start with a strong statement about the pursuit of happiness.

«»

"Ask yourself, What do we want in the country, above all? People want to be happy, isn't that right?"

Ray Bradbury, Fahrenheit 451

What Happiness Is Not

We usually like to be right rather than wrong, although there are occasions when we wish we had been wrong about our assumptions.

«»

The attraction of cynicism was that it so often put you in the right, as if being right led directly to happiness.

Richard Russo, That Old Cape Magic

We are often told or tell others or ourselves that "it is all relative." Even if we pick a reasonably relevant comparison, is it all that comforting?

«»

It has not yet been recorded that any human being has gained a very large or permanent contentment from meditation upon the fact that he is better off than others.

Sinclair Lewis, *Main Street*

The context for the metaphor in this quote is a man's moving out of the house where he and his deceased wife lived. The metaphor is very powerful.

«»

It's no good going on living in the ashes of a dead happiness.

Nevil Shute, *A Town Like Alice*

Thinking too much about whether
we are happy or not is likely to be
counterproductive.

«»

*It doesn't seem useful to think about whether
you are happy or aren't.*

Diane Johnson, Lulu in Marrakech

Here is another admonition about
overthinking the happiness goal.

«»

*…we're not happy, we don't know why, and
we drive ourselves loony trying to get better.*

Richard Ford, *Independence Day*

This plea comes from a recently deceased
former wife appearing to her
erstwhile husband.

《》

*"Well I go on asking myself, why can't people
be happy, poor dears? Why do they have to go
moiling and toiling and worrying each other?"*

Joyce Cary, *The Horse's Mouth*

Here is some very good advice from a
prolific author who is a favorite of mine.

«»

*"Half the unhappiness in the world comes
from people trying to be someone else."*

Louis Auchincloss, East Side Story

Limits on Happiness

Do we need to be able to explain
happiness in order to have it?
Let us hope not.

«»

Happiness is something we cannot explain.

Willa Cather, *The Professor's House*

This is a very perceptive and philosophical comment about not only our capacity for happiness but also about the limits of our financial status in affecting it. The quote comes from a favorite book I read in the seventies.

«»

However, in the end I did discover what some rich people never discover—that we all have a certain capacity for happiness and unhappiness. And that the economic hazards of life do not seriously affect it.

John Fowles, *The Magus*

Assuming we have a reasonable capacity for happiness, it may not come unfettered by other emotions. Is this contradiction more common than we would like?

«›»

"I am not used to happiness....It makes me afraid."

Jean Rhys, Wide Sargasso Sea

Even if all seems to be going "swimmingly," we may not be as happy as we had hoped. The irony here is jarring.

«»

One should always beware, however, of worldly contentment. C. G. Jung once treated a couple for severe neurosis brought on by nothing but the perfection of their life.

Piers Paul Read, *A Season in the West*

And even as we sense rare moments of
pure happiness, we suspect that they
may not last.

《》

*We experience such happiness only once or
twice in a lifetime, when we believe (usually
falsely) that all our troubles are finally
behind us and the future will be what we
always hoped.*

Linda Grant, The Clothes on Their Backs

Perhaps, we can reasonably expect only temporary and incomplete happiness.

«»

We are born innocent...we suffer terrible disillusionment before we gain knowledge, and then we fear death—and we are granted only fragmentary happiness to offset the pain.

Philip Roth, *The Professor of Desire*

I find this quote far too pessimistic.

«»

...(for there is little to tell of happiness—happiness is only itself, placid, emotionally dormant, a state adopted with a light heart but a nagging brain).

Jim Harrison, "Legends of the Fall" in *Legends of the Fall*

The context for this quote is a woman's
eminent loss of her husband, which seems
to put a limit on her happiness.

《》

*A woman had to choose her own particular
unhappiness carefully. That was the only happiness in life: to choose the best unhappiness.*

Lorrie Moore, "Paper Losses" in
Bark: Stories

This quote reminds us that there are times when we may not want to be happy.

«»

Joy does little to increase one's judgment. Happiness is not the condition you want to be in when you need to be at your most competent.

Richard Powers, *Generosity: An Enhancement*

Although there is some truth in this
quote, we may disagree with it because
there were times when we were conscious
in the moment of our happiness.

《》

*No man ever knows when he is happy; he
can only know when he was happy.*

Gore Vidal, Creation

Here is another suggestion that happiness is not in the present. It comes from an author famous for his children's books, but his adult fiction and mystery novels are excellent.

«»

"True happiness...lies only in memory or anticipation."

A. A. Milne, Four Days Wonder

Although we start with the assumption that happiness is a primary goal, it deserves questioning.

«◇»

"Bein' happy's OK in its place; but other things count more."

Jack Kerouac, The Sea Is My Brother

Here is an implied question worth asking about the value of happiness.

«»

There are more ways than one of being happy, better perhaps to be peaceful and contented and protected.

Jean Rhys, Wide Sargasso Sea

According to this quote, we have to engage in some work to obtain or retain happiness.

«»

"All happiness is fleeting. An exception, a contrast. But we have to rekindle it from time to time, not allow it to go out."

Mario Vargas Llosa, *The Notebooks of Don Rigoberto*

Here is a thought-provoking theoretical question about happiness.

«»

What if there is only an equal ratio of happiness to unhappiness in the world at any given time?

Gabrielle Zevin, The Storied Life of A. J. Fikry

This character apparently felt that he
lacked the capacity for happiness.

«»

He felt he did not know how to feel.
Eleanor Catton, *The Luminaries*

When we sense that happiness is eminent,
we should be quick to embrace it.

«»

*...they felt almost happy, in that melancholy
way in which happiness sometimes chooses
to manifest itself.*

José Saramago, *The Cave*

My extensive reading of literary fiction bears out this idea that fiction addresses more unhappiness than happiness.

《》

...it takes only a modest talent to write about misery—and misery is a more congenial subject than happiness. Most of us have known some suffering and can understand and respond by filling in the gaps. But great happiness is almost incomprehensible, and conveying it in print requires genius.

Paul Theroux, *Hotel Honolulu*

Why are our memories so full of unhappy matters and short of happy ones?

«»

I remember I was happy. Is it not a curious irony that we should recall our miseries with such plainness, and that our happiness should pass over us so indistinctly that, when it is gone, we can scarcely realize that it ever existed?

W. Somerset Maugham, *The Making of a Saint*

What Happiness Is

Maybe happiness is as simple as this.

«»

I do all right. I like birds, I like women, I like language. These foolish things gladden the heart.

E. L. Doctorow, *City of God*

Can it be as uncomplicated as this, at least for those of us who like to talk?

«»

"...telling about things is one of the great joys of life."

Primo Levi, *The Monkey Wrench*

I am very fond of this humorous but perceptive suggestion that some rather simple things can give us happiness.

«»

Never underestimate how much assistance, how much satisfaction, how much comfort, how much soul and transcendence there might be in a well-made taco and a cold bottle of beer.

Tom Robbins, *Jitterbug Perfume*

I would not have thought of this as a
recipe for happiness.

«»

*I can think of nothing pleasanter than to
be close to danger or discomfort, but still be
protected, preferably by one's own foresight
and effort.*

Wallace Stegner, All the Little Live
Things

This reminds me of the advertisements that tell us that "getting there" is more satisfying than being there.

«»

We're shaped to think the things we want will make us happy. But shaped to take only the briefest thrill in getting. Wanting is what having wants to recover.

Richard Powers, *Generosity: An Enhancement*

Here is a reminder that we need not be conscious of our happiness; it may be an unconscious state.

«»

Happiness consists of living in the dailyness of life and not knowing how happy you are. True happiness comes of not knowing you're happy, it's an animal serenity, something between contentment and joy, a steadiness of the belonged self in the world.

E. L. Doctorow, *Andrew's Brain*

This is a lofty and optimistic perspective about joy, which is related to happiness.

«»

Joy is a permanent and stable raising of the spirit—of a spirit that trusts in its own goodness and truth.

John Hersey, The Conspiracy

Here is another recipe for joy, one that contrasts it to wisdom.

«◊»

...real joy consists of knowing that human wisdom counts less than the shimmer of beeches in a breeze.

Richard Powers, The Overstory

This character is discussing with a friend her new-found feeling of belonging after having spent her life "on the outside looking in."

《》

The feeling that bubbled up so richly inside her, filling her, drowning her, exhilarating her, had to be happiness!

Louis Auchincloss, *The Lady of Situations*

How many of us find that happiness
may sneak up on us?

«»

*It was funny. How if a thing went on long
enough it got different. It got to be a way of
living, and you did not remember any other
way, and this way had its own happiness, too.*

Robert Penn Warren, Meet Me in the
Green Glen

I heartily agree that those who are fortunate enough to love their work are most likely to be happy. I was very lucky to love (most of) my work.

«»

"…loving your work (unfortunately, the privilege of a few) represents the best, most concrete approximation of happiness on earth."

Primo Levi, The Monkey Wrench

Here is a notion about happiness that
might be surprising.

«»

*"One can be happy and miserable both at
once, you know."*

Elizabeth Goudge, Green Dolphin Street

From the same author and book, comes
an idea with which we may need to
struggle to appreciate the truth of the
seeming contradiction.

«»

"To be sorry and glad together is to be
perceptive to the richness of life."

Elizabeth Goudge, *Green Dolphin Street*

One of my favorite authors delves into the meaning and content of happiness.

《》

He merely thought that life without happiness is impossible. What was happiness?... Looking forward was happiness—that's all—nothing more. To look forward to the gratification of some desire, to the gratification of some passion, love, ambition, hate—hate too indubitably. Love and hate. And to escape the dangers of existence, to live without fear, was also happiness. There was nothing else.

Joseph Conrad, Under Western Eyes

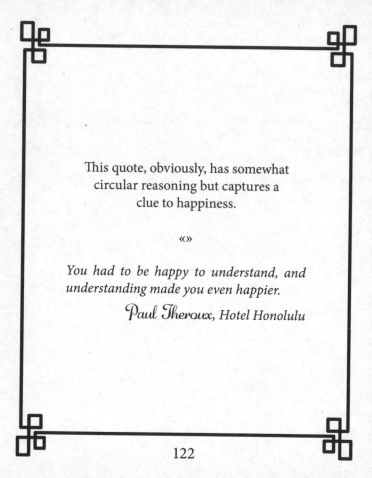

This quote, obviously, has somewhat
circular reasoning but captures a
clue to happiness.

«»

You had to be happy to understand, and
understanding made you even happier.

Paul Theroux, Hotel Honolulu

Here is a rather philosophical idea of what makes us happy.

«»

And that's what makes men happy, believing in the mystery and importance of their own little individual lives.

Willa Cather, *The Professor's House*

A great deal of our likelihood of finding happiness is determined by our own outlook and perceptions.

«»

I had found what I was looking for—a man like myself, but one who in his search for meaning had discovered a worthwhile object for his life; who had paid every price and not counted it a sacrifice; who was paying it still and would pay it till he died; who cared nothing for compromise, nothing for his pride, nothing for ourselves or the opinion of others; who had reduced his life to the one thing that mattered to him, and was free.

John le Carré, The Secret Pilgrim

Here is another and briefer notion that we are masters of our capacity for happiness.

《》

...nothing has any value outside the inner life, the silent self.

Carlos Fuentes, The Eagle's Throne

How to Obtain It

Could it be that some or all of us are predestined to have happiness?

«»

"I believe that paradise is ordained for happiness; and that men will be indulged in it according to their dispositions and gifts."

James Fenimore Cooper, *The Last of the Mohicans*

Even when we are dealt setbacks, it
is up to us to make the best of the
circumstances.

«»

*Maybe she was happy. Some people managed
to be, despite all manner of ill fortune, just
as a great many of the world's fortunates
somehow contrived to be miserable.*

Richard Russo, *Bridge of Sighs*

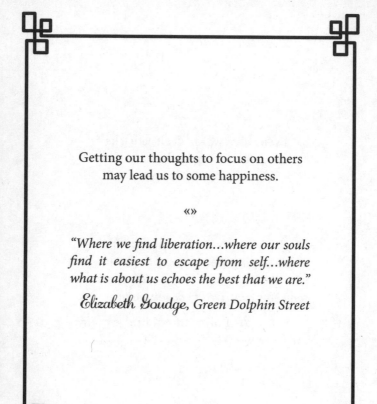

Getting our thoughts to focus on others
may lead us to some happiness.

《》

*"Where we find liberation...where our souls
find it easiest to escape from self...where
what is about us echoes the best that we are."*

Elizabeth Goudge, Green Dolphin Street

The author who claimed work as the key to happiness suggests that alternative endeavors may also offer us good prospects for happiness.

«»

"I really believe that to live happily you have to have something to do, but it shouldn't be too easy, or else something to wish for, but not just any old wish: something there's a hope of achieving."

Primo Levi, *The Monkey Wrench*

So, we must take our happiness whenever
and wherever it finds us.

«»

*Watching her lifted me into a comparable
state of happiness. As if it had arced brain
to brain. This was pure, unreflective,
unselfconscious emotion. It had taken me
by surprise and was almost too much to
bear—happiness.*

E. L. Doctorow, *Andrew's Brain*

Do we accept this as the formula for happiness or should we insist that we can and do have happy memories?

«»

If the human race didn't remember anything it would be perfectly happy.

Robert Penn Warren, *All the King's Men*

Here is a route that the wise person can take to achieve happiness.

«»

"...a man is happiest when there is a balance between his needs and his possessions. Now the question is: how to achieve this balance. One could seek to do this by increasing his goods to the level of his appetites, but that would be stupid. It would involve doing unnatural things—bargaining, haggling, scrimping, working. Ergo? Ergo, the wise man achieves balance by reducing his needs to the level of his possessions. And this is best done by learning to value the free things of life: the mountains, laughter, poetry, wine offered by a friend, older and fatter women."

Trevanian, Shibumi

This quote offers a stereotypical and exaggerated, and perhaps contrary, idea about the happiness of rich and poor.

«»

"Rich people are never happy…but poor people are happy practically without exception."

Halldor Laxness, Independent People

Our expectations about where we think
we will find happiness may limit our
finding it.

«»

*There are pleasures to be found where you
would never look for them.*

Marilynne Robinson, *Gilead*

This quote from one of my favorite authors reminds of us of our need to be alert to the prospects for happiness.

«»

One thing I did learn from Freud, which has never diminished and has indeed grown with the years, is a habit of careful observation, of heedfulness, in my relationship with the rest of the world. To learn to see what is right in front of one's nose; that is the task and a heavy task it is. It demands a certain stillness of spirit, which is not the same thing as a dimness of personality, and need not be partnered with a retiring, bland social life.

Robertson Davies, *The Cunning Man*

If we can control ourselves and deal
constructively with our flaws, we should
be more likely to find happiness.

«»

*That if a man can learn to swallow pride and
to live with shame, then he is possessed of
greater power to realize his hopes than many
another who values the world's estimate.*

George Garrett, *The Succession*

Here is another suggestion about our predisposition to find happiness.

«»

And so he came to realize that there were two kinds of people: those who were curious about the world and those whose shallow attentions were pretty much limited to those things that pertained to their own well-being.

Tom Robbins, *Fierce Invalids Home From Hot Climates*

This character is confident of
his contentment.

«»

*"I would never give myself up to the place
or to any other place. I'm the place. I guess
that's the reason. I'm the only place I need."*

Don Dellilo, *Ratner's Star*

This is an interesting question about happiness that would not have occurred to me.

«»

But what if it isn't a "luxury?" What if it's a necessity, a dirt-poor necessity? The conscience, I suspect, is a vital organ. And when it goes, you go.

Martin Amis, House of Meetings

Conclusion

Some amount of money is a key goal for most people. For others a key goal is wisdom. In each case, however, their ultimate goal may be happiness. It is relatively easy to say that money alone is not guaranteed to produce happiness. There may be more of a question about wisdom's ability to make us happy. It would not be unreasonable for people to try to have more money or wisdom to see if either helps make them happy. In any case, it is clear that literary fiction has a lot to say about these goals and how to achieve them.

Reading this book will likely not help readers make money. It may provide some small bits of wisdom. In any case, I hope it will contribute to my readers' happiness.

I would like to express my deep appreciation for Tyson Cornell's enthusiastic support and creative ideas for this third volume of my quotations, and for the hard work by all of the staff at Rare Bird, including Alice Marsh-Elmer for the development and execution of the excellent design, inside and out, of the book; Hailie Johnson; Guy Intoci; and Alexandra Watts.

Thanks to Cara Lowe for the illustrations.

Visit michaelrossauthor.com